T0353179

JOE WHITE

Joe is a graduate of the Royal Court Young Writers' Programme and Invited Studio Group. He was previously a member of the BBC Writersroom 10, and recipient of the Channel 4 Playwriting Award. In 2015 he was the Writer in Residence of Pentabus Theatre Company, and in 2017 he was selected for the Old Vic 12 and Orange Tree Writers Collective. *Mayfly* is his debut play.

Other Titles in this Series

Joe White

MAYFLY

NICK HERN BOOKS

London

www.nickhernbooks.co.uk

A Nick Hern Book

Mayfly first published in Great Britain in 2018 as a paperback original by Nick Hern Books Limited, The Glasshouse, 49a Goldhawk Road, London W12 8QP

Mayfly copyright © 2018 Joe White

Joe White has asserted his right to be identified as the author of this work

Designed and typeset by Nick Hern Books, London
Printed in Great Britain by Mimeo Ltd, Huntingdon, Cambridgeshire PE29 6XX

A CIP catalogue record for this book is available from the British Library

ISBN 978 1 84842 734 1

Mayfly was first performed at the Orange Tree Theatre, Richmond, on 19 April 2018. The cast was as follows:

LOOPS	Evelyn Hoskins
BEN	Simon Scardifield
HARRY	Irfan Shamji
CAT	Niky Wardley

Director	Guy Jones
Designer	Cécile Trémolières
Lighting Designer	Christopher Nairne
Sound Designer and Composer	Jon Ouin
Costume Supervisor	Megan Rarity
Movement	Jennifer Jackson
Casting Consultant	Juliet Horsley CDG

Acknowledgements

First and foremost, I'd like to thank Guy Jones for pulling me from the river, and Paul Miller for believing in us. To Evie Hoskins, Irfan Shamji, Simon Scardifield and Niky Wardley, for being better than I could ever imagine, and Oscar Crowe, George Pocock and Ryan Layden for appearing from out the blue. To Cécile, Jon, Kit, Bessie, Emily, Dominique, Sara-Lee, Jenny, Megan, Becs, and everyone else at the Orange Tree, who have made this so joyous. To Nick, Laura and Maeve at The Agency, and John and Sarah Liisa at Nick Hern Books. To everyone who has helped during the development of the play, but mostly Elizabeth Freestone, Simon Longman, Tim Foley, Ella Hickson and Matt Jessup. And to my friends and family, for all the love and support – not least: Alex, Hannah, Mum and Dad, who are there always, and whom I love unreservedly. Thanks for bearing with.

J.W.

For Katie, Laura and Nick,
who performed all my early plays
in our living room. I love you.

'Each day is a little life: every waking and rising a little birth, every fresh morning a little youth, every going to rest and sleep a little death.'

Arthur Schopenhauer

Characters

LOOPS, *twenty-five*
HARRY, *twenty-seven*
BEN, *forty-five*
CAT, *forty-six*

The play is set in the heart of Shropshire, on a Sunday in
early May.

Note on Text

/ indicates overlapping dialogue

– at the end of a line indicates an interruption. One in the
middle of a line is a shift in thought, or a change in tack

(dialogue in brackets is up for grabs, but probably not said)

*This text went to press before the end of rehearsals and so may
differ slightly from the play as performed.*

LITTLE BIRTH

One

First thing.

HARRY *pulls* BEN *out of the river.*

BEN *coughs up a lungful of water.* HARRY *hits his back.*

HARRY *wears a waiter's uniform, but no shoes or socks.* BEN *has his shoes on. Both men are drenched.*

HARRY. That's it, that's it, just…

> BEN *rolls onto his side, coughing, breathing, waving his hand: 'I'm okay.'*

Jesus. Fuck. I thought you were… Are you hurt?

Good, no, nor me. You sort of, elbowed me, in the balls, few times, but that's fine, I'm fine, that's fine, just an accident.

…

Sorry it, took a while to… I had to take my shoes off. And socks. They were, like, sixty quid. The shoes. Got you, though.

> HARRY *pulls his shoes to him. Inside are his socks, and his phone.*

Should I phone an ambulance, or… Like… Family, or –

BEN. Don't have one.

HARRY. Okay.

Okay, well. Let's just sit a minute, then. Watch the. River – Cos, you know, you can still. Drown? Even now, like, even on dry land, your lungs can. Fill up –

BEN. I'm fine –

HARRY. Yeah, just saying, is all. Pretty grim. Drowning on dry land… Think I'll put ma socks back on… Ma socks and shoes…

S'alright, down here, ain't it. River and that. When you're not in it. Little… what's it… Dragonflies, and that. S'alright.

Beat.

BEN. your dad never take you fishing.

HARRY. Uh… My… Uh, no. He did not.

BEN. Mayflies.

HARRY. Hm?

BEN. Them. Only live a day.

HARRY. Oh.

BEN. Hatch in the morning, mate in the afternoon, die at night. That's it.

HARRY. That's it, huh… *Huh.*

BEN. what?

HARRY. Just. Amazing what can happen, in a day, ennit. In *one* day. 'Mazing. How much can change –

BEN. Jesus Christ –

HARRY. What?

BEN. okay –

HARRY. I don't –

BEN. I just slipped. Alright. I was walking too close to the edge, and I – I just slipped in –

HARRY. right –

BEN. So, that's – so, you don't need to –

HARRY. All I was / saying was –

BEN. / You don't need to say this stuff, okay? At all. Alright?

HARRY. Alright.

> HARRY *takes a sodden pack of cigarettes from his pocket. Squeezes them out. Puts the cigarettes back.*

BEN. Anyway, I should probably –

HARRY. Yeah, I don't know how to…

BEN. What?

HARRY. I was here, mate. Whole time. I watched you, I was *shouting*, at you, you must have –

BEN. I don't –

HARRY. You didn't slip. I watched you. Wade in. Close your eyes, open your (mouth)… You didn't slip. You were. Careful. And, you know, I don't even walk to work? Normally, to – I work at The Bear, the pub, up –

BEN. Mm –

HARRY. And, on the few occasions when I do – when it's light, now it's spring, if it's dry – I, I, go along – I walk up there. Through the field. I never come down here, at all, not ever, so you need to understand something: this morning, for whatever reason –

BEN. I understand –

HARRY. Let me talk. This morning. *Something*. Is like. *Looking* – It's like something *wanted* me – like something is looking out for you. Or something. And wanted to use me to – *Use* me – And you can't even give me the courtesy to just –

BEN. okay –

HARRY. to just say: 'things aren't that bad', and, and 'a lot can happen in a day' –

BEN. alright –

HARRY. I don't know what I'm doing, okay, I said we should watch the river a minute ago – I don't want to watch that fucking thing, do I? I've just been in it. It's freezing. But I was panicking –

BEN. Okay –

HARRY. I'm still panicking –

BEN. Yes –

HARRY. And you elbowed me in the balls on purpose. I know you did –

BEN. *Alright*. Jesus Christ. Alright…

Look… uh…

HARRY. Harry.

BEN. What?

HARRY. My… Sorry, you – you left that gap there / for me to say –

BEN. / No I was just –

HARRY. Well, it sounded like –

BEN. I don't want to know your name.

HARRY. Fine. / What? That's rude, I just saved your life.

BEN. / I just – Listen.

I don't… actually, remember. I… was walking and then… I just… found myself in there. In the… It's like my mind just… Stopped.

HARRY. Are you – Have you taken something?

BEN. No. No, it's just this place. This morning. Something else.

You ever been down here before? To the bank down here. There used to be a swing. In the tree, up there – tyre swing – long time ago. Long time. From when I was little. Everything else is the same.

HARRY. Oh, I don't know. What's that, uh… 'No man ever steps in the same river twice. For it's not the same river. And he's not the same man'… Sorry –

BEN. It's okay –

HARRY. I don't know what I'm –

BEN. No. Well, that makes two of us.

BEN smiles to HARRY. *BEN stares at him, as if something has just twigged.*

HARRY. What?

BEN. No, just, you remind me of someone, a bit.

HARRY. Do I?

BEN. ...Or maybe it's the, uh – Maybe I'm seeing things. You know, I did swallow a fair bit of water there.

HARRY. Mm.

BEN. Nearly drowned there, probably. Actually.

HARRY. Mm.

Pause. HARRY *nods and stares out.*

BEN. I think I should go now.

HARRY. okay.

BEN. I only live (up there).

HARRY. Right.

Cool –

HARRY. What you doing with the rest of your Sunday?

BEN (*almost laughing*). Uhm. I dunno. What's a man s'posed to do after –

HARRY. Yeah, I dunno.

BEN. Watch football, maybe.

HARRY. Right.

BEN. Though I follow Aston Villa. So. I'll probably be back down here in an hour. That was a joke.

HARRY. Oh –

BEN. You not into football?

HARRY. Not at all.

BEN. No. Well. Neither are Villa, really.

HARRY. Do you want me to, like, walk with you, or –

BEN. I'm fine. Sorry about your uniform. And your fags.

HARRY. S'alright. They'll kill you, those things… There's a-a lost-and-found box at the pub, so… And we're closing anyway –

BEN. The Bear?

HARRY. Hm?

BEN. They're closing The Bear?

HARRY. Mm. Terry's moving to town. Sold it to some posh twat from Wolverhampton. Gonna turn into an art retreat or summin, I heard.

BEN. Jesus.

HARRY. I know, just what we need. Retreat, I'll make 'em retreat… That's what Jez said. The chef. Sounded better from him. We had a leaving party last night. 'Bout six people came.

BEN *offers his hand*.

BEN. I'm sorry.

HARRY. S'alright, less cleaning for me to do today –

BEN. No, about…

HARRY. Ah right. Yeah. 'Bout that. Well. Yeah… Hope you don't drown later, on dry land.

BEN. I'll try not to. Bye. Harry.

BEN *leaves. A moment.*

HARRY. What the fuck –

Two

LOOPS *is there, dressed in full camo. She has writing all over her arm – black pen. She has a red dress with her.*

LOOPS. I don't feel much. Like, I've never cried, in all my life, not ever, not even when I was a baby, ask my dad, doctors did all these tests on me. Weeks and weeks, but concluded I was just hard as fuck. Doctor said 'this baby's just hard as fuck' and tossed me back to Dad...

LOOPS *changes into the red dress.*

There's only a handful of times I can remember feeling anything at all. But one of them was with you...

She sighs. Maybe she reads something on her arm.

I know you don't remember me. I'm not. Memorable, but I remember you. And feeling. Something. Feeling... fucking hell, this is shit...

Maybe no words. Maybe, just. Walk up to 'im, like.

She does what she thinks is a cool nod.

And then... just... then...

LOOPS *makes a fist. Holds it up to her face. Looks at it. Leans in.*

Remember me?

LOOPS *kisses her fist. With tongues. It shakes a bit. She holds it with her other hand. Stops kissing. Holds her hand. It shakes and shakes. She tries to control her breathing.*

BEN *appears.*

BEN. What are you / doing in here?

LOOPS. / Fucking hell, you trying to fucking kill me, / you jeb-end?

BEN. / What are you wearing?

LOOPS. What, I don't know, a dress –

BEN. Your mum's dress –

LOOPS. No it isn't –

BEN. Yes, it is –

LOOPS. Yeah it is, so what, why you wet?

BEN. Loops –

LOOPS. Why are you wet, Dad?

Beat.

BEN. …Ha. Yeah. Ha. Funny story, actually – you'll laugh at this – listen to this – I just went for a walk, right –

LOOPS. A walk?

BEN. Just now, down by the – I do like walking, Loops – in the. Woods. By the river.

LOOPS. …

BEN. And, and – it's, uh – you'll laugh at this, really – I was standing at the edge, there, right – wait for this – you know, where we used to have that – and I was just –

LOOPS. Dad –

BEN. Looking at the, at the *tree*, there –

LOOPS. Dad –

BEN. Our initials, there, and, and my footing just – Like the bank just… completely gave way, fat bastard, and I, I, I just –

LOOPS. Dad.

BEN. mm?

Pause.

LOOPS. Are you alright?

BEN. Yeah. Yes. Course.

Why are you in my shed, Loops?

LOOPS. Why are you in your shed?

BEN. Because I've got some gardening clothes in here –

LOOPS. Oh, gardening clothes, / you gonna garden now, after your walk –

BEN. / And rather than traipsing through the house, soaking wet –

LOOPS. Just normal behaviour –

BEN. Oh, and what about you? In that. Huh?

LOOPS. What, I wanted to try it on, so what –

BEN. In my shed –

LOOPS. It's not like she's gonna wear it, is it –

BEN. Loops –

LOOPS. What?

Beat.

BEN. Just. Budge out the way, will you…

BEN *pulls out some dirty gardening clothes.*

There y'are. See? We can both play dress-up.

LOOPS. I'm not playin' dress-up.

BEN. This shed was your first barracks, weren't it –

LOOPS. Dad, I'm not playin' dress-up.

BEN. No? Then what's all this about, then?

Beat.

LOOPS. I was thinking about… doing something. Special. Later –

BEN. Special?

LOOPS. Special dinner. Maybe. For tonight. Seeing as it's –

BEN. Mm. Mm –

LOOPS. Haven't eaten together in ages. So, I got… from the Spar. In town. Last night.

BEN. Town... How did you get all the way to...

LOOPS *has a plastic bag, full of plastic containers.*

Curry.

LOOPS. Yeah, I thought, with my boyfriend coming over, and –
They're they're reduced, so –

BEN. What?

LOOPS. They're reduced.

BEN. No, boyfriend?

LOOPS. Yeah.

BEN. *Boyfriend?*

LOOPS. Yes, Dad, boyfriend, Jesus Christ Almighty, well, he
doesn't actually know he's my boyfriend yet, but it's going
to happen –

BEN. Sorry, who is... what –

LOOPS. Just some guy, wicked guy, we went to cadets together,
alright –

BEN. Cadets.

LOOPS. He's local.

BEN. Obviously –

LOOPS. And he understands me better than anyone, in the
whole world, so –

BEN. In the whole world?

LOOPS. Any more, yeah. I think. I want to do something, Dad,
I have to, today. What's this face about?

BEN. What face?

LOOPS. Yours, mate. All...

BEN. Shut up. I don't have a face –

LOOPS. Gormless –

BEN. Shut up.

LOOPS. You're looking at me.

BEN. Yeah, cos. You look…

LOOPS. What?

BEN. Womanly, or something –

LOOPS. *What?* Fuck off –

BEN. I don't know –

LOOPS. 'Womanly', you fucking jeb-end –

BEN. No, just –

LOOPS. 'Womanly.'

BEN. Just like your mum, I mean. Like she used to look. Give us a spin then –

LOOPS. Fuck off.

BEN. Okay.

BEN *looks her up and down, and nearly laughs.*

No, I think it – it just dawned on me. This is the first time I think I've seen you out of your camouflage in…

LOOPS. Yeah, well, that's sort of my job, Dad, I kind of need to / wear it.

BEN. / I know, I know. Just. Proud, or something –

LOOPS. Proud?

BEN. Or something. You know. Not that you need to wear a dress to get a boyfriend, darling –

LOOPS. Worked for Mum, didn't it. Got you when she wore this. And if she could do it. You know…

BEN. Yeah. Yeah, right then, Loopy Lou, out you get. I need to change my trousers.

LOOPS. And? I've seen it all before.

BEN. What?

LOOPS. Yours, I mean – seen yours – loads, it's like, mahogany-coloured, innit, like you borrowed it from someone –

BEN. Louise, Jesus –

LOOPS. What? That's good innit? That I haven't seen anyone else's?

BEN. I don't want to talk about this –

LOOPS. Fine.

BEN. Thank you.

LOOPS. Right.

BEN. Go on then.

LOOPS. What?

BEN. Leave.

LOOPS. Now?

BEN. Yes. Stop stalling.

LOOPS. Alright, alright, I'm going… Gonna go… Get me a boyfriend. See me another todger –

BEN. *Just go –*

LOOPS. Yes, fine, I'm gone. I'm already gone…

BEN *smiles and starts to undo his belt.*

You think I look alright then?

BEN. I think. You look better than your mum ever did, in that.

And that he's a very lucky guy. Whoever he is.

LOOPS. Well, obviously. Thanks.

Three

The kitchen.

The video is on – kids playing in a river.

BEN *holds the plastic bag full of microwave curry. He has waterproof trousers on. He watches* CAT, *who has a phone and a magazine.*

CAT *dials a number. It rings. It clicks. The voicemail of a young man – mid-twenties – can maybe just be made out.*

CAT. Hey, babe. Hope you're good, and, uh… I know what you – I know your thing about ringing you… but I was reading my stars, just now, and – yeah, stars again – but I read this bit, and it – listen to this – stopped me in my tracks, this, says: 'Today A very special person will appear. From out the blue…' Today. Of all… So I thought I'd give you a ring. In case you fancied… whatever… Cos. I wanna see you, babe. Come see me.

She hangs up. Pause.

BEN *pretends he's just walked in.*

BEN. Beautiful day out there.

CAT.…

BEN. The light, and… Spring… You'll never guess what. Louise is wearing your dress.

CAT. what dress?

BEN. What do you mean – Your dress. *The* dress.

CAT. She got into it?

BEN. What?

CAT. It's tiny.

BEN. Well, yeah, well, yeah, well, I was just telling you cos – You know… She was out of her camo gear –

CAT. her camo –

BEN. Yes, for the first time in God knows –

CAT. A year.

BEN. And she's bringing a boy round, tonight. A boy*friend*. Apparently –

CAT. A boyfriend?

BEN. Yes, a boyfriend, don't sound so shocked –

CAT. who?

BEN. I don't know. Some lad from somewhere. She's gone to ask him out right now –

CAT. In my dress?

BEN. She wants to be like her mum. She said –

CAT. She wants to be like everyone in this family, Ben, 'cept herself –

BEN. Cat, Jesus Chri– She's trying to do something, okay, she's trying to… She wants us to have dinner together. Meet a new – She's trying to. Defibrillate us, I don't know…

CAT. Defibri… well, fucking hell, that's a big word –

BEN. What?

CAT. This is the most you've spoken in a year, Ben –

BEN. A yea– Don't be / ridiculous –

CAT. / To me. Yeah. And you come out with words like… That… You been reading the dictionary all year, have you. (Fucking hell.)

CAT *watches the video.*

BEN. It means –

CAT. I know what it means.

BEN *watches her. He laughs a bit. Then doesn't.*

Silence.

BEN.…'Parently, they've… They've sold The Bear. 'Parently.

CAT. What?

BEN. Some dingle from Wolverhampton. Gonna turn into a fuckin' art retreat or something –

CAT. Jesus.

BEN. I know yeah – Retreat, I'll make 'em fuckin' retreat.

CAT. We should go.

BEN. To the art centre?

CAT. To The Bear.

BEN. I think – They had a leaving party last night –

CAT. So?

BEN. And, you know, maybe – You know maybe today isn't the best –

CAT. So, wait, let me get this straight… Louise can have her first ever boyfriend round today –

BEN. Come on –

CAT. But we can't go and say goodbye to our pub?

BEN. Look –

CAT. Our pub, Ben. This video, earlier, I was watching, this boy. You should have seen him, stood up in that pub. Saturday night. Packed full. Stood up on a table, singing for everyone, singing his heart out, thinking he was Bruce Springsteen or someone, can't have been older than seventeen, that hair –

BEN. Bandana.

CAT. All the girls watching him, up there. Everybody watching. And this one, in the far corner. Could hardly see her, she was that little, in the dark, in that dress, watching that boy, no idea what's ahead. Just there. And happy. And in complete… awe…

BEN. Not at the singing –

CAT. No, Jesus Christ, never at the singing.

BEN *smiles*. CAT *doesn't*.

'Magining the man he'd be. Life they'd have.

BEN *goes to peck* CAT, *but she does the tiniest movement away, and he stops.*

Pause.

Any nice plants coming up?

BEN. Hm?

She looks him up and down.

Oh. The – Yeah, uh – Few things. The… mock orange, at the back… And the lilac, that's starting to come through –

CAT. That's nice.

BEN. Yeah.

CAT. Nice you're back gardening.

BEN. Yeah.

CAT. Like old days. Almost.

CAT *watches the tape.* BEN *watches her for a few moments.*

BEN. Are you not… punishing yourself, darlin'. Watching…

CAT. No?

BEN. Cos you're not gonna suddenly see something you didn't see before –

CAT. I'm not looking for something I ain't seen before, Ben…

One from cadets here. Marching band. You remember?

BEN. Mm.

CAT. Got it from the bedroom. You should see the dust in there. S'like a bloody smoke grenade's gone off, bloody tonnes of it… And. You know. All of it. The dust. Pieces –

BEN. I'll give it a hoover –

CAT. That's not what I'm saying –

BEN. I know. But maybe it's… Spring clean, you know. Time –

CAT. Not today, can't today, told you, we're going to The Bear –

BEN. Cat –

CAT. What? You don't have to have a drink –

BEN. I – I know that –

CAT. Just do something, Ben. For me. You're doing something for her –

BEN. We won't know anyone –

CAT. You don't know that. Someone might just… appear. You don't know.

Beat.

BEN. I'll drop you up there. In a bit. But I… I won't –

CAT. fine –

BEN. Promise you won't get pissed –

CAT. No.

BEN. Then promise you'll try with this boyfriend tonight.

CAT. whatever –

BEN. Thank you –

CAT. S'not for you –

BEN. I know. But. Anyway…

BEN *goes to put a hand on her shoulder. Doesn't.*

CAT. One year, eh.

BEN. Mm.

CAT. 'One day at a time…' That's what they all say. In all my (magazines). Idiots. Every day's the same. Ennit.

BEN. Not today, darling. Got a feeling 'bout today.

Four

*An hour or so later. The beer garden in The Bear Inn. Maybe
a 'GOODBYE' or 'THANK YOU' sign somewhere. Maybe
balloons, deflated. Cigarette butts, bin bags.*

LOOPS *in her red dress and boots.*

HARRY *in a pair of very tight shorts, and a baggy uniform
shirt. He holds a bin bag.*

LOOPS *doesn't look at him much.*

LOOPS. You don't remember me, I'm not – I'm Lou, we met at
    Army Cadets, ten years ago – you don't remember, that's
    fine – I don't cry, uh. Ever. Doctor said I was hard as fuck, so
    – as a baby – so, yeah, don't feel anything, at all, never have,
    'cept this one night, with you. You don't remember, that's –
    It was last night of cadets. Camp. The boys sneak into our
    dorm, cos the girls want to play this game thing, where you
    have to guess where our nipples are. Guess our nipples and
    belly buttons. With our pyjamas on. Which is erotic, and
    challenging, cos we're all different aren't we? Some people
    have really, like, low, nipples, or whatever – And anyway,
    you're paired with me, cos no one else – I guess maybe
    we're getting bullied, you seem upset, you don't want to do
    it, you look at the floor, and you just sort of jab your finger at
    me, and turn to go, but you… You get it. You get me. Bang
    on. My left one. I think you feel it. And I say 'wowza'. Like
    that. Breathy. 'Wowza.' And people cheer, cos – Maybe
    they're bullying still, but I don't care cos it feels real, like in
    a rom-com, and you have this. Smile. I notice it. And then
    you guess my right one. And you get that too and – I s'pose
    that's easier after the first, cos you sort of line 'em up, don't
    you, I wouldn't know – and then I nod, and then your hand
    moves down, to my stomach. And you look me in the eye,
    for the first time… and I didn't mind looking in yours, uh…
    sorry… hang on… Uh… 'Bomb… sound effect…' No, that's
    not yet, sorry. Sorry. Uh… So…

She looks back to her notes.

Oh yeah… so… Then, really gently this time, your hand reaches – Your finger just (moves), like that, and, like, slowly dis-disappears into me, into my stomach, my belly. Only up to about there, and with a pyjama. Sheath. Over it – shouldn't – don't say sheath – but, it feels like you've reached right in. Your whole hand. And touched something, right in the core of – Freezing cold in the core of me… and, just for a second… lit it up. And, it's like…

She makes an explosion sound effect. A moment.

And then I sort of… ran out of room there, but basically, anyway, I know you don't remember me or anything but I was thinking that was the best bit of my life, so far, probably. I know it is. I never really realised before. But I've had a shit year, and I'm trying to do something, and I've missed you. I've realised I've missed you. And I'm back for a couple of weeks now – Off tour – I've been – so I thought I'd look you up. Today. And see what you were up to. And see if you remembered that too, and whether you might wanna. Have dinner. With – Do you like curry? It's reduced but it's fine. Sorry… Sorry –

HARRY. No.

LOOPS. Fuck's sake –

HARRY. No, that was… Did you – Sorry – Did you say Army Cadets?

LOOPS. Yeah.

HARRY. Yeah, I thought so… Uhm. This is – I – I don't know – I'm really sorry – I didn't go to Army Cadets… I've never… I'm a pacifist, so –

LOOPS. Oh.

HARRY. I went to, this, like… shitty, like, Blue Peter camp, once? Summer camp. When I was fifteen. For a couple of days. But that was in Droitwich Spa or somewhere –

LOOPS. Yeah, no, that's – that's it.

HARRY. Oh. I didn't realise that was. Army-related... I spent my whole time making puppets out of felt.

LOOPS. It was definitely army-related.

HARRY. Right, yeah...

Beat.

LOOPS.…It's okay. I knew you wouldn't remember me, anyway, I just. Wanted to try…

Okay –

HARRY. It's not… Thing is. I-I blanked a lot of that stuff out, around that time. My dad, sort of… I remember, actually, the build up to that. It had been non-school-uniform day? At the end of term, we didn't live – Like we were living in town then. And, and, anyway, I… I accidentally went in wearing my – my mum's jeans – They – they looked *exactly* like mine, okay, colour-wise, folded up, 'cept they were – I didn't realise till I got in – But they were a bit flared at the bottom… and there was this tiny, like, butterfly, on the bum pocket. Done in, like, gems, like diamante gems, and anyway, the girls laughed and the boys battered me, and my dad found out, and I – I guess the blokes at the pub were – Cos he went proper mental, this time. Kept saying I had to 'straighten out', kept saying he was gonna 'straighten me out'. And my mum was – It was one of the weeks she was in her room, so, anyway, he sent me to that camp. I guess he thought it was army-related as well –

LOOPS. It was.

HARRY. Yeah. And anyway. The lads who battered me went to that camp too. So I just got battered there, instead of in school. For a whole week.

LOOPS. Oh.

HARRY. Yeah. 'Was a bit of a bloody nightmare.'

HARRY *laughs*. LOOPS *takes the cue, and laughs too*.

No, it really was a nightmare –

LOOPS. yeah, no –

HARRY. Yeah. Amazing. At the time, I thought. End of the world. And then. Totally forgotten. Till now.

LOOPS. Sorry –

HARRY. No, no. As you can tell, it worked wonders in the long run… I'm sorry, I'm not… 'the man you hoped I'd be…' Hah…

LOOPS. …hah…

HARRY. I can't imagine how scary that was for you. To do that. Just walk out here, and –

LOOPS. Yeah. Well. I'm pretty hard.

HARRY. Right, yeah.

LOOPS. The hardest thing was saying it to you in your shorts without laughing –

HARRY. These aren't my shorts.

LOOPS. No?

HARRY. No, Jesus, these are lost-and-found.

LOOPS. Lost-and-found.

HARRY. Yeah, some dickhead, earlier, in the woods… like…

LOOPS. What?

HARRY. …Uh… just… like –

LOOPS. *What?*

HARRY. Like. Just. Stole my trousers. And shirt.

LOOPS. Really?

HARRY. …yeah.

LOOPS. The shit.

HARRY. It's okay, no one died.

LOOPS. Wish I was there.

HARRY. Yeah. Yeah. Anyway. I'm sorry I don't, uhm. I wish I remembered that night, in the dorms. I wish I remembered you.

LOOPS. That's okay. I look different now. Some say. W-womanly. So –

HARRY. It's the dress.

LOOPS. What about it?

HARRY. No, just, you look. You're. Really. Uh. Pr-pretty? And… 'I'm not very good at this.'

LOOPS. No.

HARRY. No.

LOOPS. But I wouldn't be either. Without my notes.

HARRY. 'Nipple soulmates.' On your arm.

LOOPS. Oh, you saw that, did you.

HARRY. I did, yeah. Soon as you came out here, really. Pretty big handwriting.

LOOPS. Yeah. You must think I'm…

HARRY. No, not today. Normal for today. Did you guess mine right, by the way? At camp?

LOOPS. It was boys on girls, really. Way of the world.

HARRY. Do you want to… have a go now? So it's fair?

LOOPS. Uh –

HARRY. No, uh – Sorry, that was… ''Twas a stupid idea.' Ha. ''Twas.' Twat –

LOOPS. It was, yeah –

HARRY. Yeah, 'twas, yeah –

LOOPS. So, what do you think about tonight?

HARRY. Oh. Uhm. Yeah. I was – I was gonna do this. Work. Thing.

LOOPS. I thought you were closing today?

HARRY. Yeah, no, it is, we are, I mean after I finish cleaning up –

LOOPS. What work thing?

HARRY. It's out towards… It's a bit of a drive –

LOOPS. Well, I'll come with you. I like cars. Then we go to mine after.

HARRY. Uh –

LOOPS. Cool. Could be cool. You could pick me up. If you like. In your car. Take my phone number. Gimme your phone. Please. Ha.

He does. She puts her number in.

So, yeah. Cool. Cool. Good day. And night. Feels good. That's me.

HARRY. Yeah.

LOOPS. Shall I keep this on? For later? You've got my phone number now and it's not very comfortable.

HARRY. I mean. Maybe something, like, more outdoorsy, I guess?

LOOPS. Like my camouflage?

HARRY. Your… Oh, you still – You're in the actual Army now –

LOOPS. First Battalion, Royal Irish, mate. Up in Tern Hill.

HARRY. Right. Cool. Well, yeah, your camo is – I guess, in a way, it is a bit of a mission, so –

LOOPS. I love missions. So you call me, yeah?

HARRY. Yeah.

LOOPS. Yeah. Cool. See you later.

LITTLE YOUTH

One

The Bear's beer garden. Two hours later. Mostly cleared up. White sun, middle of the sky.

CAT *is sat, drinking from a huge glass of wine, and smoking.* CAT *takes out her phone, dials, waits.*

CAT. Hey babe. So, I'm at The Bear. Having a glass of my favourite. In the sun.

Must have missed the party.

She hangs up. She downs all but the dregs of her drink, dials again, and waits.

Hey babe. You'll never guess what. They're closing The Bear. Yeah. Selling it to some dickhead from Wolverhampton. Having a big party, everyone's here, getting pissed, you should see it. That barmaid you shagged is here. You did shag her, didn't you? On a birthday or something, she's gorgeous. God, I feel... I feel really great, babe. So nice to get out, have a drink... Remember that time your army mates asked me for a gang bang? Cheeky buggers. I remember slapping that one round the face. And you, you looked at me, like... What did you look at me like? You remember? Or did I ask them? Memory, eh. Good old days...

She drinks.

You know. My horoscopes said. That today. Said, today, you'd... So, I figured. If anywhere. Maybe. You'd come find me here...

HARRY *enters with a tray of glasses behind her.*

CAT *closes her eyes.*

Babe, I need to tell you something.

When I close my eyes… I, uh… I can't…

HARRY *reaches for the bottle on her table. She opens her eyes to see him.*

HARRY. Sorry. Was just grabbing –

CAT. Oh, yeah, hang on.

CAT *downs the dregs.*

There.

HARRY. Thanks. Uh. We're about to close –

CAT. Are you new?

HARRY. Me? No, I've, I've been here a year now, nearly –

CAT. A year? That long?

HARRY. Nearly.

CAT. Just shows you. We used to come a lot.

HARRY. Oh, right. (*Showing his badge.*) I'm Harry.

CAT. That says Phillip.

HARRY. Oh yeah. This is Phillip's badge. Phillip got out while he still could –

CAT. I'm Cat. Or whatever. Whatever you want.

HARRY. Cat's a good name. I, uh… like cats. Who doesn't? Well, loads of people, s'pose. Allergic and that –

CAT. What are you going to do for a job? Now this place is – Sorry if that's –

HARRY. No, uh, I should have sorted myself out by now, to be honest. I've been – this place has been crumbling for years. Maybe find something in town. Like. 'Nother pub, or something. Betting shop. Got loads.

CAT. Town.

HARRY. Yeah.

CAT. You got a car then?

HARRY. Course.

CAT. I never learned. Can you believe? Out here. Stupid. Always liked being driven, was my problem. Always had someone to drive me – Town's good.

HARRY. Jobs, ennit. Few.

CAT. People. That's the best thing. People. Don't get people out here no more. Nearest people are when a plane flies over.

HARRY. I don't know. What's that quote? 'People are hell', or something. I don't know. I don't even know who said it. Some guy –

CAT. Some guy talking out his arse, it's the opposite that's hell – D'you want a fag?

HARRY. Uh, no… I'm…

CAT. Well, sit with me while I have one, will you? Last day and all, they won't care. Don't make me beg, babe.

HARRY. Uh. 'Kay. Just a minute, though.

HARRY *sits. A few moments.*

CAT. You know. Every man, I ever loved, was here.

HARRY. Oh.

CAT. Pathetic, ennit. One grotty little pub, middle of bloody nowhere. About to be forgotten for good. But they were. All here… Handsome, aren't you.

HARRY. Ooh. No. Not really.

CAT. You got dark eyes.

HARRY. Are they.

CAT. In the middle.

HARRY. Well, I guess they all are, aren't they, in the middle. Pupil –

CAT. Shouldn't have stopped coming here. Could have got to know each other.

HARRY. I, yeah, I-I keep myself to myself, really, most the time –

CAT. Dark and mysterious, eh.

HARRY. No, no, Just. Like being out the way, I guess…

CAT.…Bet you get loads of girls after you.

HARRY. Oh, no. Never.

CAT. Never?

HARRY. Well. You know. No.

CAT. Would have thought you'd have them swarming around. Whole village.

HARRY. Whole village, ha. Whole village is about ten people. And they're all ancient.

CAT. Are we?

HARRY. Uh, well, no, not – not you, you're, you're, you're –

CAT. Yeah, finish the sentence, please –

HARRY. Young – you're young –

CAT. Oh, you, charmer. How old do you think I am, then?

HARRY. Uhm… Like… Like… Thirty-/nine?

CAT. / Charmer –

HARRY. or so –

CAT. I'm forty-six.

HARRY. Well, yeah, that's… The average round here is, like, like, double, like, triple that, so… No kids. That's the problem.

CAT. What?

HARRY. My dad says. No natives. Just rich, old people, replacing each other. And when that happens, places like this just become… places you drive past on your way to somewhere else. Ghost towns. Makes us the ghosts, you know –

CAT. Okay –

HARRY. Sorry, I'm –

CAT. Talking shit –

HARRY. Yeah.

CAT. S'alright. It's the right day for talking shit, I suppose –

HARRY. Yeah –

CAT. Well, look, you can fuck me if you want –

HARRY. What?

CAT. If you wanted to. No big thing, in the toilets, or whatever, find a bush –

HARRY. Uh –

CAT. Little farewell of our own, eh –

HARRY. I've got a girlfriend.

CAT. I've got a husband.

HARRY. Look, that's a very – It's – That's flattering, I'm flattered, really, wow, wowza, but –

CAT. Jesus Christ, calm down, I'm only fucking joking, mate.

HARRY. What?

CAT. I'm just fucking with you. Jesus. Calm down.

HARRY. Oh –

CAT. Just a joke.

HARRY. Right, yeah, good one –

CAT. You're sweating.

HARRY. Yeah.

CAT. You're like properly sweating.

HARRY. A bit, yeah.

CAT. You never had someone fuck with you before?

HARRY. Yeah, course I have –

CAT. You want some spray or something?

HARRY. What?

CAT. Do you want some spray? Cos you're all sweaty? I got some. If you want it.

CAT goes to her bag retrieves a small can of deodorant.

HARRY. What, like... uh... It's for men?

CAT. They don't make this one any more. Rare.

It's pretty old, but if you give it a shake it will...

I'm okay, thanks.

CAT. Girls will be all over you with this, babe.

HARRY. Look, really, I'm – I'll be alright, thanks, thank you, though. I've got to go now –

CAT. Yeah, right, okay, me too –

HARRY. Cos we're actually, like, officially / closed now?

CAT. / yeah, no, I'm going too, I was waiting for someone, but... Don't' think they're coming, anyway. Bastard. Fucking – Ha. Ah well.

She puts the can away.

Sorry to gnaw your ear off –

HARRY. No, no. Hope you... Hope you feel better.

CAT. Ah. Hah. Yeah.

HARRY. You never know. I... I'm – I feel lonely. Usually. But. Today. Out the blue... So. You never know.

HARRY *starts to go.*

CAT. You think. I know this sounds… You reckon, if you closed your eyes. In a few minutes' time, in an hour's time, say, if you closed your eyes, do you think you'd remember what I looked like?

HARRY. Uh. I think so, yeah.

CAT. Would you?

HARRY. I think so.

CAT. No. Would you. Do that? In a bit? In a few hours' time, maybe, just… Just close your eyes, and. Is that. Oh God, you're looking at me like I'm –

HARRY. No. Uh, sorry, I –

CAT. It's okay. Least you're looking… Ha. Fuck. What do I fucking sound like –

HARRY. I can do that, later. Yeah.

CAT. Thank you. That would really make my day.

Two

The bedroom. Tiny. Filled with dust.

A cardboard box is open on the floor.

BEN *packs things away.*

He finds a mobile phone. Tries to turn it on. It doesn't work. He finds a plug. He charges it.

He packs more things away.

He finds an Aston Villa shirt – his, once. He folds it. He smells it.

Three

*On top of Clee Hill. Late afternoon. Very high. We hear the
wind. Huge purple sky.*

HARRY *wears a garish shirt (brand new – with packaging
folds), smart trousers and walking boots. He has writing on
his hand.*

LOOPS *wears her camo.*

HARRY. Pretty high up, eh? Yeah, I think I read somewhere it's
– (*Reading his hand.*) the seventh highest peak in England, at
over five hundred metres –

LOOPS. It is, yeah. Highest land eastwards until the Ural
Mountains in Russia.

HARRY. Yeah –

LOOPS. That's why there's a pub over there called The Kremlin
Inn. Some dickhead trying to be funny, I s'pose. I guess it's
funny if you're a dickhead with no sense of humour.

HARRY.... You know it then?

LOOPS. Oh yeah.

HARRY. Is that true? The Russia stuff?

LOOPS. No, I'm making it up to impress you. Course it's true.
Used to come up here a lot with my family. Can see miles
some days. Bit misty now, but that's not your fault. That way
– west – you've got Snowdonia, and the Brecon Beacons,
and the Black Mountains. That way – south – are the
Malvern Hills, and the Cotswolds. Over there – north – on
a very clear day, the peaks of the Peak District. And there...
East... Kidderminster.

HARRY. And then, after that, the Ural Mountains.

LOOPS. My brother was conceived in that bus stop over there.

HARRY. What? Really?

LOOPS. So the legend goes. Night my mum and dad met.

HARRY. Right.

LOOPS. Their first date, too.

HARRY. …Ha… Lucky your mum and dad aren't celebrities, ennit, or they'd have named him Number Forty-four, or something… uh –

LOOPS. They thought they were, at one time. Celebrities – in the village, anyway. Like most people in villages do. Nice being known I guess, if you care about that shit.

HARRY. And what about you?

LOOPS. I don't care about that shit.

HARRY. No. Do you know where you were. Made.

LOOPS. Oh, just in a bed, at home, I think.

HARRY. Right, yeah, same.

LOOPS. Not special. They needed a little plaything for him. Loads of fucking sheep is the problem here, ennit, I hate fucking sheep, don't you, / stupid twats –

HARRY. / Not really.

LOOPS. Nah, s'pose they're alright, really, if you like stupid fucking blank fucking stares all the time.

HARRY. Reminds me of that painting. You know. With the boy in the water. He's been flying, or something, and he fell, and it's the moment after he hit the sea, and you see his little leg, there, disappearing in – and all these blokes, these farmers and that, and all these sheep are just carrying on, staring blank, like nothing happened… which, I guess, it didn't, to them.

LOOPS. Right…

HARRY. 'In the countryside, no one can hear you scream.'

LOOPS. Yeah.

HARRY. Yeah.

Beat.

We could scream. If you wanted.

LOOPS. Why would we do that?

HARRY. Yeah, I don't know. Cos, kind of… rom-com thing to do, I s'pose.

LOOPS. Stupid.

HARRY. Yeah, stupid, just joking, just mean, like… People think that cos you're from a small village, that everyone will know you. But we can still go missing. Out here. Even right next to each other… S'like you in your camo, ennit. Blending in –

LOOPS. I wear the camo cos I'm in the Army, mate.

HARRY. Yeah, no –

LOOPS. Why else would I wear it?

HARRY. Yeah, no, yeah, just, even when you're not on duty?

LOOPS. I'm proud of it. Proud to wear it. Reminds me. Always. So why are we on this fucking hill then?

HARRY. Oh. Uhm, so –

LOOPS. I'm hungry –

HARRY. No, yeah, we won't be long – So, we're going… mushroom-picking… Uh –

LOOPS. you joking?

HARRY. hm?

LOOPS. Mushrooms?

HARRY. Yeah. But, but cool ones. Uh. Psilocybins. Magic mushrooms. This is a hotspot.

LOOPS. Clee Hill?

HARRY. Yeah – What, you don't know?

LOOPS. No.

HARRY. Oh big time. Yeah, big time, big time, big time, they even put police up here some nights. In mushroom season. Packing heat.

LOOPS. What?

HARRY. Jez told me. The chef at the pub. Told me he'd pay me shitloads if I could get him some. They're good for depression, 'parently, I dunno –

LOOPS. Right. Whatever.

HARRY. Yeah, and, anyway, apparently, last year, police were, like, roaming about up here, with, like, machine guns and that.

LOOPS. What, SIGs?

HARRY. What?

LOOPS. That's the automatics the police use here. They're massive.

HARRY. SIGs, yeah. Lethal.

LOOPS. Hell yeah. Cut you in half.

HARRY. Got you going now, ain't I?

LOOPS. That all true, yeah?

HARRY. No, I'm just making it up to impress you.

LOOPS. You ever seen someone get shot?

HARRY. Have I –

LOOPS. Or die in any way?

HARRY. …Uh…

LOOPS. So. You're a virgin, then. Death-wise.

HARRY. Oh, yeah, death-wise, I am.

LOOPS. And how d'you feel about it?

HARRY. What?

LOOPS. Death.

HARRY. Oh, death. Uh. Same as most people, I imagine. Just try not to think about it. Day to day. Sort of hope there's something else. After. Not sure there is –

LOOPS. There ain't. Sorry to tell you, but, sooner you know the better, really. No ghosts, no angels –

HARRY. No. None of that. I reckon the people who say that stuff – on their deathbeds and that – people who say they can see loved ones or angels or whatever. I reckon they're only saying that for us, you know… That they can't see anything at all. S'only then they realise. And they spend those last few moments. Lying. Pretending. So *we* can feel alright. Which is just…

LOOPS. Stupid –

HARRY. Amazing. I think…

LOOPS.…I thought I saw a ghost once, but it was just a bin bag in a tree… Anyway, what are we looking out for then? Mushroom-wise?

HARRY. Uhm. Well. Sheep shit, actually.

They start looking.

The shrooms will be near that stuff, but not in it or on it, so, uh, you know, don't go fingering some turd for nothing… What we're looking for are liberty caps. They're, like, this big, browny-yellow, and have thin, bell-shaped –

LOOPS. And after we get them, we go back to mine, yeah?

HARRY. Yeah, but, but listen be careful, cos they are these ones, which look exactly like 'em, called death caps.

LOOPS. Death caps?

HARRY. Yeah, but, don't worry, it's just a name. Well, some people die. But, look, uh… whatever you do, you know, just ask permission before you put anything in your mouth.

LOOPS.…okay.

HARRY. Okay. Do you copy, soldier?

LOOPS. Don't take the piss.

HARRY. No, sorry.

LOOPS. Right. Sheep shit. Sheep. Shit.

They look around, looking at each other now and then.

Fucking mess everywhere, ennit. Plastic and shit.

HARRY. Gets blown up from the car park and that down there –

LOOPS. Will make 'em choke won't it, the sheep, not that I care
cos I hate the woolly twats, but –

HARRY. Desperate to leave our mark, ennit. Be remembered.
Pff.

They search a bit.

LOOPS. You sound like someone. A bit.

HARRY. Do I?

LOOPS. Yeah. You getting paid a lot for these then? If we find
any…

HARRY. Uh, yeah. Yeah, a fair bit. But was thinking, like,
I might keep a few. For me and my dad, like. Be mad, that.
See shit. And. He gets. Like. Down. Sometimes. So. Just
trying something new. Been looking last few days –

LOOPS. No luck yet?

HARRY. Not yet, no. Thought there might be some down by
the… by the river, but, uh –

LOOPS. Wait. Is this one?

HARRY. Let me see… Uhm… Oh, yeah, I think – Yeah, I think
it is, hang on…

HARRY *compares it to a photo in his pocket.*

YES. Yeah. Wow, Louise, that's – there are actually loads
here – that's amazing – Get you, Queen of the…

LOOPS. Whatever.

HARRY. You're a natural.

HARRY *half-hugs* LOOPS. *She smiles. He stares at her.*

LOOPS. What are you looking at me like that for?

HARRY. Sorry. I, I didn't realise I was –

LOOPS. No. It's… You can carry on.

HARRY. Okay.

HARRY *looks at her a bit more.*

Uh… Uh… *So.* So. I'm just gonna… uh… excuse me… if I may… just…

He kisses her. A sort of half-peck, which misses most of her mouth. Then he goes in again. She closes her eyes. They hit each other's teeth. They try to snog a bit. It's awful. LOOPS*'s hand starts shaking. She holds it. After a few seconds,* HARRY *notices it, and steps back.*

Sorry.

LOOPS. I'm fine –

HARRY. Your hand –

LOOPS. I'm fine, it's fine, do you wanna do it then? The mushrooms? Let's do one.

HARRY. What?

LOOPS. We could, right now, I want to, If you do, I don't mind, might be nice.

HARRY. Okay.

LOOPS. Okay.

HARRY. Okay.

LOOPS. Okay.

She eats one.

Four

The bedroom. Tight spotlight. Some time later.

The phone lights up, alive. BEN *goes to it. He holds the shirt. He listens to a voicemail. We can just make out* CAT*'s voice.*

He deletes the voicemail.

He listens to another. He deletes that one too.

And so on and so on, until…

CAT *is stood in the doorway, watching him. She is wearing the red dress.*

CAT. Ben.

BEN (*snapping back to life, hiding the phone*). Yeah? Yes?

CAT. What are you doing?

BEN. Oh, just –

CAT. I phoned you.

BEN. Did you.

CAT. Had to walk back.

BEN. Sorry.

> BEN *pockets the phone. Maybe* CAT *sees. If she does, she hardly reacts.*

> Is that her dress?

CAT. My dress –

BEN. Your dress –

CAT. It was under her bed.

BEN. Oh. Maybe she changed her mind.

CAT. Amazing you fell for this. Tatty little thing. Millions of years old.

> Can still get into it.

You know, you do this thing. You been doing this thing for a year. It's what they tell you to do to dogs when you're punishing them. Dogs and kids. You don't look 'em in the eye. Make 'em feel invisible. You do that to me.

BEN. I don't mean / to –

CAT. / Can't even look at / me now.

BEN. / Sorry. Sorry…

BEN *looks at her. They stare at each other.*

D'you see who you were looking for? At the pub…

CAT *shakes her head. A while of them staring at each other.*

CAT. You cleaned.

BEN. Mm.

CAT. Found your Villa stuff.

BEN. Yeah.

CAT. D'you smell it?

BEN. (yeah)

CAT. Worn off now. I got the last of it. Last bit.

She taps her temple.

Louise not back then –

BEN. She won't be long.

CAT. Right… You know I could have gone with anyone. Back then. But I only wanted you. I still do… What I'm sayin' is. Last orders, Ben. Ringing my bell… Why don't you come have a drink with me –

BEN. What?

CAT. What?

BEN. Cat, don't ask / me that.

CAT. / Oh, don't look all wounded –

BEN. Why would you – You know not to ask me –

CAT. It's just one drink, you're not gonna suddenly lose it on one –

BEN. It wouldn't just be one drink, that's the point –

CAT. Fucking hell, do you even know what today is?

BEN. Of course I do. And I want to be there for Lou, and sober and –

CAT. It's not her fucking night, Ben –

BEN. No, it's our night –

CAT. It's Adam's night. It's our son's night.

Whose night is it?

Ben?

Say his name.

Please. Say Adam…

Just say his name, Ben, just once, in here. Cos he – He might – You don't know, he might – He might hear *you*. So. Please. Darling. Please?

Please.

Please –

BEN. Cat –

CAT. I can't remember what he looks like, Ben. Without the videos. When I close my eyes. I can't. Conjure – I can't see him any more, and that terrifies me. Cos I think. If I can't see him, if I've forgotten him, then maybe he's forgotten me, too… And I'm left with you. Who can't see me either. So what am I? I'm dead, too. Aren't I. I'm dead.

I'm going to have a drink. Look at my boy.

Five

Clee Hill. Night falling. Deep violet.

LOOPS *and* HARRY *are eating mushrooms.*

HARRY. These are pretty rank, actually.

LOOPS. Mm.

HARRY. Absolutely fucking disgusting, really.

LOOPS. Yeah.

HARRY. I can't feel anything, neither –

LOOPS. I never feel anything.

HARRY. Like, not even like, less depressed or anything, like nothing –

LOOPS. Got to give it time, ent you.

LOOPS *eats another and immediately spits it out.*

That's a bad one.

HARRY. So, you – you alright now, then?

LOOPS. What?

HARRY. Your… hands and that.

LOOPS. Yeah, fine, completely, just a bit cold up here. Shake sometimes. When it's cold.

HARRY. Is that bad, like, for Army, and that? Like when you're holding a gun.

LOOPS. Nah. Solid as anything when I'm holding a gun, mate. Steady as a rock…

HARRY. Yeah, I'd be shit in the Army. Probably die my first day. Loads of the lads from school joined. Good money, I s'pose. Escape and that. And better than working in town, ennit, in a pub, or the Spar, or a betting shop, and what else is there? Couple of farms left. The abattoir. Fuck that. Army, or what? No wonder we all fucking…

LOOPS. How's it s'posed to feel when they kick in?

HARRY. Uh. Like. Flying. Like flying, mixed with… like… cool colours and… uh, yeah, I've never actually done it before, so I don't know –

LOOPS. What?

HARRY. Always wanted to. With the right person. Like. Always liked the idea of seeing stuff.

LOOPS. What stuff?

HARRY. I don't know. Just. Stuff we can't normally see.

LOOPS. Like what?

HARRY. I don't know, just stuff.

LOOPS. Like ghosts.

HARRY. No, just –

LOOPS. We're not going to see ghosts, Harry –

HARRY. No, I know that – I don't think we're going to see anything, actually, cos, I can't say for definite that they were all liberty caps, so –

LOOPS. What?

HARRY. So, so – yeah, I think they were – but, maybe we should go to hospital or something –

LOOPS. Harry.

HARRY. I'm panicking.

LOOPS. Yeah.

HARRY. I know it's not cool –

LOOPS. We'll be fine.

HARRY. I'm not some cool stud muffin, Louise –

LOOPS. Look at me. Harry –

HARRY. Not some Army boy –

LOOPS. Look.

> HARRY *does*.

> We'll be fine. Okay?

HARRY. 'Kay.

LOOPS. And if we're not fine. You know? There are worse places to die.

HARRY. what?

LOOPS. Like. Like. Being crucified. Or burning to death. Or drowning. Must be shit –

HARRY. Trampled –

LOOPS. Yeah, good one –

HARRY. By sheep.

LOOPS. Yeah, fuck that.

HARRY. fuck that.

LOOPS. Or just at home, surrounded by family, that would be a fucking nightmare. There are loads of worse ways. Aren't there. Like. Fuck it. I think. I think if this is it. Here. Today. With you. You know? I've seen a lot of types, you know, not – Not crucifixion. Or trampled by sheep. But pretty much everything else. S'what Army's good for. Learning 'bout that. Dyin' young. It's like upsetting nature, or something, ennit? Like not doing what our bodies tell us, what time tells us, like getting killed for something bigger than time and bodies, which is actually dying for us. Centre of it all, centre of the universe, 'Fuck You God', I'm in control, you know?

HARRY. So, you mean, you're in the Army so you can… like… die?

LOOPS. Kind of.

HARRY. So. Like. Suicide / then?

LOOPS. / What? No. What?

HARRY. Well –

LOOPS. It's with glory.

HARRY. Yeah. No. But it's still sort of – It's by proxy, isn't it. Suicide by proxy –

LOOPS. I don't know what that is.

HARRY. Like, you just get someone else to do it for you. Like Jesus. Or whatever.

LOOPS. I got Jesus to kill me?

HARRY. No, like he got someone to kill him. He got Judas to kiss him, and all that –

LOOPS. Yeah, I don't really give a shit about Jesus –

HARRY. Fine, no, neither do I –

LOOPS. Then why do you know so much about him?

HARRY. I dunno. My mum used to talk about him a lot –

LOOPS. Yeah, well, it's all bollocks, mate, sorry.

HARRY. I know. Obviously –

LOOPS. All of it. Bollocks that people say to make you feel better, but it's still bollocks –

HARRY. I didn't mean to upset you –

LOOPS. You haven't –

HARRY. I clearly have, your hands / are –

LOOPS. / I've been near death a bunch of times, mate, and you, you know what? There's no fucking noise, or light, or change in the atmosphere – there's no Jesus or any other glowing motherfucker – there is *nothing*. There is just a hole where someone was, and there's you, breathing into it. You understand me?

HARRY. Yeah.

LOOPS. Good.

HARRY. But I don't agree.

LOOPS....what?

HARRY. I don't agree with you. There's a lot that happens. We just can't ever know it. You know.

LOOPS. Oh fucking hell –

HARRY. I'm talking about science here. I'm talking – First rule of thermodynamics, right, says the energy in the universe will always be a constant. Forever. Whatever happens. The same. It won't change when people die, or stars get sucked into black holes... So, so, so when *we*... die... that energy inside us, inside everything, just... Finds somewhere else to go... cos energy is like this... this river, right. Flowing on and on, forever, this giant invisible river, through everything, and every now and then, something leaps out of it and becomes *something* for a bit, solid, has a... little life... before it... falls back in... becomes the river again. Carries on flowing... And that's it. That's how I see it, anyway. Now... My mum. Few years ago. That stuff helped.

LOOPS. I didn't –

HARRY. I don't talk about it much. No one asks.

CAT *in the kitchen, staring at her phone.*

BEN *is stood in the doorway, watching her.*

CAT. Just. Pick up. Pick up. Pick up. Pick up –

BEN *holds the side of her face. There's something menacing in his eyes. His hand moves to her jaw, and under, to the top of her throat. He kisses her. They kiss in the blue light of the video. She puts her hands on his hands and squeezes. They stop kissing.*

CAT *exits.*

LOOPS. I try to forget him. The boy. I watch war films, play PlayStation. Try to lose that body in all of it. Muddy it up with other faces, and limbs. But you can't, really. Ever. And every now and then he hits me... out of the...

As LOOPS *talks,* HARRY *disappears.* LOOPS*'s shakes grow throughout.*

This boy. With a shaved head. I knew him, I knew him, but
he looked different. He was blue. His face and his lips and
everything, blue, everythin' 'cept his eyes, which were
r   red   He was   He was in
the air   He was up – He was hanging in the air, there.
One morning. Must have been there hours, all night, and I
pulled him down, and he fell on the ground there, and the
sound that made   M-Makes me   AH-Hollow
thud   No air in him   And I called for He was just
looking up at the   one of his eyes had   there was
soil in one, on the white, and I wanted to wipe it out, I
wanted him to blink   and the woman   on the phone
told me to give him CPR   CPR till the medics – CPR
so I tried so I I I did that, and it was the first boy I'd ever
kissed so lips were weird anyway and the woman on the
phone told me to keep going, and press his ribs even though
even though I was telling – even though
I told her he was – sheshe she just told me to stay calm and
k-keep going, and I did, for what felt like a whole day, a
whole day kissing that dead blue boy till they got there
A man and a woman And I knew them but they looked
different And then more people came and they put the boy in
a bag and took him away and I didn't ever see him again in
real life or dreams or anything cos that don't exist and after
that I stopped I stopped getting out of bed or eating or getting
dressed all of us all of us just stopped for a very long time
for a very long time until today until –

LOOPS *can't breathe. She is staring at something.*

Mayflies swarm.

A YOUNG MAN *appears.*

*He is wearing an Aston Villa shirt. He looks up for a long
time. He wipes his eye.*

He disappears.

LOOPS *is in the dark. She is drifting in and out of consciousness. She is moving fast. Her hair is moving in the wind. We hear a car, speeding, and…*

HARRY'S VOICE. You're alright, Lou. We're nearly home –

LOOPS. Adam… Ad –

HARRY'S VOICE. Nearly home…

LOOPS *fades into the darkness. The sound of the engine fades into the swarm of mayflies.*

LITTLE DEATH

The kitchen. Late. Hot. Windows wide open. Brilliant white moonlight. We can hear the river in the distance – the mayflies falling back into it.

A few lit candles. Sickly blue light from the video. An electric hum, like insects buzzing. Videos on the table.

BEN, HARRY *and* LOOPS *are all stood there.*

LOOPS *is leaning on* HARRY, *trying to focus.* HARRY *is staring at* BEN.

A long silence.

HARRY. I don't –	BEN. What happened...	LOOPS. I'm fine, just a bit sick,
	Why were you sick?	no big deal –

LOOPS. Car sick, I'm fine.

BEN. His car?

LOOPS. Yeah.

BEN. You ent been car sick in years.

LOOPS. We were going fast.

HARRY. Not that fast.

BEN. He's your boyfriend –

LOOPS. Nearly, yeah – Dad, Harry, Harry, Dad, I'm going to the toilet, sorry about your shirt.

HARRY. It's – it's alright, it's old.

She exits.

Pause.

It's not old, it's brand new –

BEN. What the fuck is going on?

HARRY. I don't know, I'm literally –

BEN. What did – Did you say anything?

HARRY. No –

BEN. You didn't say anything about this / morning –

HARRY. / I was on a date, mate. Chatting about someone trying to kill themselves isn't / exactly the sexiest thing in the world –

BEN. / Oi, keep your fucking voice down.

CAT (*entering*). Right, where's / this boy then? Jesus.

HARRY. / Oh my fucking God.

BEN. What?

CAT. What?

HARRY. What?

BEN. Do you know her – Does he know you?

CAT. No.

HARRY. No.

BEN. You just swore –

HARRY. I, yeah, I – I – I served her. You. At the pub, today – / you don't remember – you do remember –

CAT. / Oh yeah, he served me a wine, yeah, that's right –

HARRY. Wine, yeah, that's – White wine, wasn't it, house white, something 'agio', pretty rough, but –

CAT. I like it –

HARRY. No, me too, it's alright, yeah, glad you… glad you enjoyed… that –

BEN. Right –

HARRY. So. So. Met you this afternoon. Never met you before.

CAT. What's on your shirt?

HARRY. Oh, this, uh –

BEN. Louise was sick.

HARRY. Yeah. Yes –

CAT. Not in here?

HARRY. No, just on me –

CAT. Good –

HARRY. I was sick as well, a bit, down – (*Re: his shirt.*) This – This is a a sort of a a 'a coming together', of sorts, if you like, I'm-I'm sure in some weird tribe somewhere this is like a a wedding vow or something – bride and groom, vomiting on each other – I'm sorry, this is weird –

BEN. Alright –

HARRY. Louise threw up and we came here, and then I recognised you and –

BEN. She'll be alright –

HARRY. It's just mad, this whole –

BEN. Alright –

HARRY. Everything –

BEN. just breathe –

CAT. Yeah –

HARRY. Mm, mm, mm –

BEN. Breathe then.

HARRY. Mm.

   HARRY *breathes out.*

BEN. Yeah?

HARRY. Yeah.

BEN. Now in again.

   HARRY *breathes in.*

And out… And so on and so forth for the rest of the night, okay? You'll be alright.

HARRY. Yeah… thank you…

BEN. Ben.

HARRY. hm?

BEN. I thought you left that gap there… for me to say my name.

HARRY. …Oh. Yeah. Ha. Very good. Hi. Ben. Harry. Harry. Sorry.

They shake hands.

Nice to meet you.

BEN. yeah.

Beat.

CAT. Well, get him a clean shirt, darling. Poor boy stinks.

HARRY. Oh, I was gonna just… drive back –

BEN. Yeah. Course. Darling.

No, don't – I'm, I'm probably just gonna shoot –

BEN. No, no. S'gonna be fine.

BEN exits. Silence.

HARRY. Small world, ennit.

CAT. Not really, just a small village, wanna drink?

HARRY. Yes, absolutely, please, God, yes –

CAT. You nervous?

HARRY. Just a bit weirded out.

CAT. Don't be. You're alright. Home now.

CAT hands him a drink.

HARRY. Thanks.

HARRY *downs half of the drink in one.*

CAT. Can put it away, can't you.

HARRY *composes himself.*

HARRY. Thank you…

She is suddenly aware of HARRY *looking at her dress.*

CAT. So I hear Louise wore this earlier. To ensnare you.

HARRY. ha. Ensnare –

CAT. Who looks better in it, do you think?

Babe –

HARRY. Sorry?

CAT. In my dress. Me or her?

HARRY. Uh… Well –

CAT. Well?

HARRY. I mean…

CAT. Jesus Christ, babe, I'm fucking with you –

HARRY. Oh.

CAT. It's a joke, yeah?

HARRY. Yeah. No. Good one. Really good joke, that's –

CAT. Jesus.

HARRY. Jesus Christ –

CAT. Another drink?

HARRY. Yes, please.

CAT *fills his drink up.* HARRY *looks at the videos.*

Long time since I've seen these.

CAT. What?

HARRY. Videos. Thought they were. Obsolete now.

CAT. Nearly.

HARRY. It's-it's nice. The house. All the way out here –

CAT. It's a shithole. Middle of nowhere, smells of pigshit, always has, it was a pig farm, before, hundreds of years, Ben's uncle, and *his* uncle, and *his* uncle, can't you smell it?

HARRY *shakes his head.*

I cried, first night we moved in here. All the pigshit and tobacco. Didn't smoke back then. His uncle did, all the time, got emphysema, died upstairs, in our bed, in that very bed, Ben's pillow still had dried blood on it when we moved in, no one had thought to – Just a thing that happens on a farm, ennit – death – Move on –

HARRY. Christ –

CAT. Sold the pigs. Fuck that. Wasn't doing that. Ben did oddjobs round the villages – houses, gardens – I worked here and there. Then Louise came along… Never liked 'em. The house. Having them inside it. Used to bump 'em about, give 'em cuts and bruises –

HARRY. 'Them' being… Adam? Is it? Lou said his name a few times in the – She wasn't making much sense but –

CAT *reaches for* HARRY*'s hand.*

Ah, uh –

CAT. I just wanted to say thank you. For being with Louise tonight. Bringing her home safe. Sort of like a big brother yourself. Aren't you.

HARRY. Yeah. Or. Boyfriend. Hah –

CAT. Did you… do it? Earlier?

HARRY. Uhh…

CAT. Close your eyes? And see me?

HARRY.…

BEN. One clean shirt.

BEN is in the doorway, holding the Villa shirt.

This is for you.

HARRY. Great. Thanks. Ben. Hey. Football.

BEN. Aston Villa.

HARRY. Oh, yeah, did-did they win today?

CAT. You like football, babe?

HARRY. Oh no. Not at all.

BEN. But you knew they were playing today?

Beat.

HARRY. uh… Sorry. Sorry, do *I* like football? Yeah. Yes. Sorry. Thought you were –

BEN. They lost –

HARRY. Ah, *fucking hell*. What a. Fucker – Right, I'll just get changed in the bathroom, then, is it – where is –

CAT. Louise is still in there.

HARRY. Oh. Yeah. Course. Course she is. Taking a while, well, I can wait –

CAT. Can't sit all night in that disgusting shirt, babe. Just do it here. We've seen it all before.

HARRY. Uh. Yeah… Yeah, no, it's just. You know. I haven't done my crunches in a while –

BEN. Don't be such a bloody jeb-end, will you –

HARRY. Yeah, no –

BEN. Man up.

HARRY looks at BEN.

HARRY.…uh… yeah…

With his back turned, HARRY awkwardly changes shirts.

Yeah. Nice. Material.

CAT *is staring at him – eyes full.*

What? Bit tight –

CAT. (Ben.)

BEN *is staring too.*

HARRY. Uh –

CAT. Look.

BEN. Yeah.

HARRY. Sorry, is –

BEN. It's good. You look good – (*Re:* HARRY*'s dirty shirt.*)
Let me take that.

HARRY. Thanks.

BEN. Another drink? Before I put the food in. Think we've got
some bubbly somewhere, ain't we? In the…

BEN *goes searching.*

CAT. You having one, darling?

BEN. Uh… I might do, yeah…

CAT. Okay.

HARRY. Uh, only a little one for me, I'll be driving / back in
a bit –

BEN. / What's that?

HARRY. I'll drive back in a bit, so –

CAT. Oh, just stay the night, babe. Have a drink, relax.

BEN. Here we are.

BEN *finds the bubbly.*

CAT. You can stay in Louise's room, if you like. We don't mind.
We get it. Don't we, Ben?

BEN.… Yeah. Yes. And, I mean, if not, we've… we've also got
a spare room…

CAT. Uh –

BEN. You'd have to excuse the boxes. But… Yeah… You should stay.

HARRY. I'll see how the night goes. If that's okay.

BEN. Course. Yeah. Let's see how the night goes.

HARRY. She really is taking a while, isn't she, maybe I should –

BEN. No, no. Cat. You go check on her. Might be girl stuff.

CAT. What?

BEN. I dunno, look, I wanna grill this young man about our daughter, okay?

HARRY. Ooh. Ha. 'Please don't go!'

CAT. Don't worry, babe, he couldn't grill toast.

BEN. Cat. Darling.

CAT. Alright. Go easy on him. Don't go anywhere.

HARRY. Ha.

   CAT *goes. Pause.*

   I didn't say anything to her either.

   About you –

BEN. Fine.

   BEN *opens the bubbly.*

   You alright?

   He pours three glasses. Then a fourth.

HARRY. Yeah. Yeah, I'm… Just. Bit mad. You know. Like I'm in. Someone else's… You know, like, not real.

BEN. Well. Here's to. Not real.

   He hands HARRY *a glass.*

   Good to see you again, kid.

HARRY. Yeah.

BEN *sips. Then drinks more.*

BEN. Fucking hell. Fuck. That is lovely, that. You tried that?

HARRY. Uh.

HARRY *sips.*

Mm. Good.

BEN. Fucking. Glorious, that.

BEN *finishes the glass.*

HARRY. Your lungs are alright, then.

BEN. Hm?

HARRY. Haven't drowned on dry land yet –

BEN. yeah, just keep your voice down a bit, / mate –

HARRY. / Oh, sorry –

BEN. I'm fine –

HARRY. Listen, I can go if this is all too –

BEN. No, no, that would. Devastate. Her. I can handle it, if you can.

HARRY. Yeah, no, absolutely.

BEN. Nice. Having another lad around. By the way, if Cat seems a little… you should know, it's this – There's this. Anniversary. Thing.

HARRY. Today?

BEN. Mm.

CAT *enters.*

CAT. She's fine. Cleaning his camo, apparently –

BEN. Drink here, / darling –

HARRY. / His –

CAT. Don't know why she's bothering. I said: 'It's s'posed to look dirty ain't it.' Thank you, petal. Cheers.

HARRY. Cheers.

CAT. Cheers, babe. Good to have you. With us. 'To a special person. Appearing from out the blue…'

BEN. She reads the horoscopes.

HARRY. Ah. Right. Uh… To your anniversary.

CAT. What?

BEN. Uh, I mentioned…

HARRY. Cheers.

BEN. Cheers. To. Him.

They drink. CAT *watches* BEN, *who takes it a bit easier this time.*

BEN *refills. He drinks and refills throughout the scene until the bottle is empty.*

You know, Cat used to work in The Bear.

HARRY. Oh?

BEN. For a few years. Long time ago now. Long, long, long –

CAT. Oi.

BEN. Back when it was great. Before the oldies started buying up. Packed. Weren't it.

CAT. to the rafters.

BEN. And there were rafters. Forty, fifty people, all crammed in there, Friday, Saturday night, steamy windows. Everyone knowing each other, buying drinks, telling the same old stories.

CAT. And kids, loads of kids, everywhere, running about, getting mixed up –

BEN. You might have been one of 'em.

HARRY. No, we used to live in town.

CAT. Oh, that's nice –

BEN. I sang. Some nights. Can you believe? Saturday nights.

CAT. What a racket.

BEN. It wasn't about the voice, Cat, it was about the stage presence.

CAT. He stood on a table –

BEN. Well –

CAT. Pretending to be Bruce Springsteen. Had a bandana an' everything, looked more like a pirate, stupid prat.

BEN. It's mad to think now, but at one point I really thought I could be somebody.

CAT. Ben.

BEN. No, like, somebody famous, or whatever. Important. Sound like a dickhead saying that out loud, but I did. You do, when everyone tells you you're good. You know?

HARRY. No.

BEN. ... well –

CAT. Then we had a kid. And everything –

BEN. I was up on that stage first time I saw her. In the corner of the pub there. Sat watching me. In that dress. In that very dress.

HARRY. What? That one? Louise's –

BEN. That isn't Louise's. It's hers. She was glowing, that night. She actually glowed. Made me feel big. Way she looked at me. And I pointed at her. Little light in the dark. Saying. 'This is for you, darling.' And it was. I only sang to her from then on.

CAT. Wish he didn't, he had a terrible voice.

BEN *laughs*.

BEN. Still my girl, ain't you. After all this time. Still my girl.

BEN *kisses* CAT. *It is much more tender than before.*

BEN *wipes his mouth, proudly.* CAT *looks flustered. But nothing compared to* HARRY.

You don't mind us having a little kiss, do you, mate?

HARRY. No. Course not. It's nice to see – Not in a weird way.

BEN. You remember what happened next, darlin'? After that.

CAT. He took me to Clee Hill.

BEN. I took her to Clee Hill.

CAT. It's this big hill, going back towards Birmingham – you must know it?

HARRY....Uh, I think so, yeah –

BEN. Highest land eastwards till the Ural Mountains in Russia –

HARRY. Really.

BEN. So, I take her up there. And I pull over. And we go sit at the bus stop there / and look at the stars –

HARRY. / We don't need to go into any – / oh you are, okay.

BEN. / See, I used to know all the stars, back then – my uncle taught me – and I wanted to show them off to her. She said she liked astrology and that. You remember this, darling?

CAT. Mm hm.

BEN. So we're sat there, and I'm... naming constellations... and I run out pretty fast, cos I know about five, so I start makin' em up, like the Duck and the Badger, or whatever, she has no idea, she's just all starry-eyed, and... lookin' at me... So we... uh... Well –

HARRY. Yeah, uh, that's, hah –

BEN. And it was...

CAT. Perfect.

BEN. Right there.

CAT. My life. What I'm here for. Made sense, all of a sudden.

BEN. And mine. And then, week or so later, she comes here, she's walking down to me with this face, and... I know it all already, I see it all. 'I'm seventeen. I'm shovelling pigshit. And I'm gonna be a dad. With her. This complete stranger.' Neither of us had, uh –

CAT. We didn't really have families, really. My mum was young as well. Wasn't ready. Dropped me off at my gran's one day, over in the village. Never really saw her again. Couple of Christmases. When I was really little. And that was that.

HARRY. Oh. That's – Sorry –

CAT. S'alright. You realise, that sometimes, all parents really are are kids with kids. No clue. So this was my chance. And I felt him, straight away, I swear I did, even that first night, I felt him in my tummy. And I knew. I loved him straight away. And nothing else seemed to matter You know?

CAT holds HARRY's hand.

HARRY. Ah. Yeah. So. Where does Adam live now then? Not around here?

Beat.

BEN. No, he's here. Just... not...

CAT. darlin' –

BEN. I'll go get Louise. 'Fore she misses her own big night –

HARRY. Oh. Uh. I can go – Maybe, I could –

CAT. No, no, she's embarrassed. She gets like this. Weird. Small. Like her father.

BEN. I'll just be a minute.

HARRY. She doesn't – She shouldn't be embarrassed about anything –

CAT. Well, she does a bit, babe. She chucked up on her first date – and first date, like, first date, like *ever* –

BEN. Cat –

HARRY. It was my first date, too. Ever. And I threw up as well, so – Look, tell her not to be embarrassed. Please. Ben. Tell her I, uh. Do. Embarrassing things all the time. This is nothing.

BEN. Okay –

HARRY. Tell her someone walked in on me once, having a poo on a train… and that I didn't even notice them, cos, I was. Wiping. Maybe don't tell her that, but tell her I don't care.

BEN. Okay.

HARRY. Thanks.

BEN. Be right back.

HARRY. Please. Thanks. Okay.

BEN *takes the phone out of his pocket – his son's phone – and places it on the table by* CAT.

BEN *exits.*

CAT *drinks her glass, and refills. She smiles at* HARRY.

Sorry. Did I say something –

CAT. No, no –

HARRY. I always ask questions when I'm –

CAT. You have a positive effect on him. I haven't seen him like this for… He could be quite romantic when he wanted to be, you know. Quite. Devastating. In his own way. All the girls. All the boys. Loved him. But he chose me.

Can I just say though, in all seriousness: You do smell, a bit, actually. Of sick –

HARRY. Oh –

CAT. Sorry to – I had to tell you. Before she came back in, wouldn't want you to –

HARRY. Yeah, no, th-thank / you –

CAT. / You'll want to sort that out before she comes back.

HARRY. Yeah.

CAT. You can use that spray. If you want.

HARRY. Oh, uh, yeah, yes, please, thank you, that would be…

CAT *looks in her bag. Retrieves the spray.*

Brilliant, thank you.

CAT. Give it a good shake first.

HARRY *does. He sprays. Nothing.*

HARRY. Oh… uh…

CAT. You have to really shake it up properly. Really…

HARRY *does again. Then goes to spray. Maybe a tiny bit comes out.*

HARRY. Uh.

CAT. Yeah?

HARRY. Uh, lit-little bit, I think, yeah –

CAT. Oh, give it here.

CAT *puts her hand under his shirt to retrieve the spray. She shakes it.*

HARRY. I-I-I think that's all / of it –

CAT. / No. Just. Hang on. I know the trick to…

CAT *shakes and sprays. Nothing. She tries again, really hard.*

HARRY. Not to worry. I'm fairly sure I got a bit –

CAT. Hang on. Oh, for fuck's sake –

HARRY. I think I got a bit.

CAT. Did you?

HARRY. Yeah.

CAT *smells his shirt. And again, a bit harder.*

Is – Is that – Do I smell better?

Or –

CAT. You're fine.

S'pose that's all used up now, then, I s'pose. Isn't it. You think I should. Throw it out?

HARRY. Uh. I guess. Yeah.

CAT. Mm. Mm.

CAT bins the spray.

She stands looking at it for a while.

She looks at the phone on the table.

Can you do something for me, babe?

HARRY. What?

CAT. Could you... I think I might have broken my phone earlier... Want to check it's...

HARRY. Oh, my phone's in my car –

CAT. Use this one.

CAT hands the phone to HARRY.

HARRY. Uh... okay –

CAT. Dial 'Mum'.

Pause.

HARRY. uh –

CAT. Please. That's what. I am. In –

HARRY. Yeah... yeah, uh... hang on...

CAT sits on the other side of the room.

A while.

HARRY dials.

It buzzes in her hand.

She looks at it, at the name ringing her back for the first time in a year.

She tries not to cry.

She half shows it to him. She takes a deep breath. She picks up. She covers her other ear.

Uh… Hello?

CAT.…Hi…

HARRY. Hi…

CAT. Hi, babe…

HARRY.…Hi…

Are you okay?

CAT.…Not really…

HARRY. Oh.

CAT. But it's great to hear your voice. I can't tell you.

Are you okay?

HARRY.…Yeah…

CAT. Good… Babe… Can you. See me.

HARRY.…

CAT. If you, Close your eyes. I'll… I'll close mine too.

CAT *closes her eyes.*

HARRY *closes his eyes.*

Can you see me?

HARRY. uh… yeah… Yeah.

A long time.

CAT. Can you… Would you just say goodbye to me?

Please?

Can you just say. 'Bye, Mum…' And tell me you love me.

HARRY *stares across the room at her. She isn't looking at him. He is crying.*

HARRY.…

   'Bye… Mum…

   I… uh…'

BEN *enters with* LOOPS. *She's wearing pyjamas and her camo jacket. Her hair is wet. She looks different, somehow. Fresh-faced, clean, tired, young – younger than ever before.*

HARRY *hangs up the phone. He and* CAT *stare at each out.*

LOOPS. Why are you wearing that shirt?

BEN. His one was – I just grabbed something nearby.

LOOPS. Dad –

BEN. It was just there, Loops. Alright.

LOOPS. What's going on?

HARRY. Nothing.

BEN (*to* CAT). You okay?

CAT. Hm?

LOOPS. Why do you look like that?

HARRY. Like what?

LOOPS. All…

HARRY. I'm not.

LOOPS. Mum?

   CAT *wakes up. Sees* LOOPS *as if for the first time in a long time.*

CAT. What, darling?

   Beat.

LOOPS. That looks much better on you.

CAT. Thank you, darling.

LOOPS. Dad, do you want to microwave the food?

BEN. Ah. Yeah. Sure.

HARRY. Can I do anything?

LOOPS. Yeah, sit down and stop being a kiss-arse. Not. That chair. There. Please.

HARRY. Okay –

CAT. Louise.

LOOPS. What? He's fine, we're fine, you're fine, aren't you?

HARRY. Yeah.

LOOPS. See?

> HARRY *sits*.

CAT. Alright.

> BEN *holds one of the microwave meals, and a fork*.

BEN. Want to hear the loneliest sound in the world?

> *He pops the meal.*

I'll just go and nuke these.

> BEN *exits*.

LOOPS. Are you hungry, Harry?

HARRY. Yeah. Starving. You?

LOOPS. Mm, yeah, I vommed loads, didn't I. What's that smell?

HARRY. What?

LOOPS. You smell of… It's nice. You staying over?

HARRY. Uh –

LOOPS. You can, if you want, whatever, can sleep on the floor if you like, like a sleepover, like camp. Don't have to sleep together. That might be weird.

HARRY. Uh.

LOOPS. Might be nice, I dunno, whatever –

HARRY. Yeah.

LOOPS. Yeah. Right. See?

CAT. Uh. Okay, then. There we go.

CAT *goes to top up* BEN*'s glass.* LOOPS *puts her hand over it.*

LOOPS. Let's not. Tonight. Yeah.

CAT.…alright, darling. Alright.

BEN *enters with some of the food, a bunch of cutlery and four plates.*

BEN. Right, here's the first two. Cartons –

HARRY. Great. I'll take those.

LOOPS. Thanks, Dad.

BEN. It was nothing, really.

CAT. Ben. Louise has just asked this young man if he'd like to spend the night.

BEN. Oh right?

CAT. And he said yes.

BEN. Okay.

CAT. In her room.

BEN.…Well. We were younger than these two when we moved in here. Weren't we. Right. Get started. Just nuking the others. Back in a mo…

He exits, singing Springsteen.

CAT. Whereabouts do you live, Harry?

HARRY. Oh, uh, not that far, actually. Like. Few miles. Out in the middle of nowhere, too. Old farm, as well, actually. Was. At some point. Little old lady owns it. Margaret. She's fun. Mad. Taxidermies animals she's run over. Keeps reading us her erotic poetry. It's terrible.

CAT. Us. Being.

HARRY. Oh, uh, me and my dad… We used to live in town, up until about… uh… three years ago… but, we had to. Move –

It's complicated, but, my mum... uh... You know. I don't –
I don't ever talk about it...

CAT. You don't have to –

HARRY. No... Doesn't mean I don't want to. Haven't wanted
to. Just. Working out how to...

BEN *enters with another couple of cartons.*

She. Went. She's. Missing? I guess. All we really know is:
she got up early, one morning, took the car. Took a few
things from home. Some photos. Of me. No note. She just...
And my dad said all sorts of things. At the beginning. For
himself, mostly, mostly – He said she was dead. And I used to
think it mattered. Knowing. But it's the same thing. Dying.
Leaving. She's just somewhere else. And we spent best part of
two years just. Competing? Shouting, crying, not crying, not
talking. I started smoking, We had a fight – We actually had
an actual fight. In the living room. Fucking hell.

HARRY *laughs. Calms down.*

I sort of won... but, you know, he's pretty old, so...
Afterwards. We were sitting there. On the floor. My dad with
a split lip. Carpet burn up his face. Shirt open Belly out. Not
his best. We're sitting there. Just staring at each other. Across
the room there. And that seemed to do it. Actually. Just.
(Looking.) Going: 'Yeah, I'm here too...' Next day we left
the house. Sold it few months later. Some old couple.
London. Next to nothing. And, then, I don't know. Got here.
Somehow... Little things. Chat. Pint. Look at each other.
Remember her. Miss her. I miss her. Every day. I have no
idea where she is. And I feel like I should hate her, but I
don't, I just miss her. And that's the only bit which never
goes away, and that's alright.

Everything is suspended. We hear insects.

Anyway, can I have the rice please?

LOOPS *holds his hand. She serves his dinner with her other
hand.*

LOOPS. You want naan?

HARRY. No. Naan for me, thanks.

No, yeah, I do, please.

You have to do it one-handed, though…

LOOPS *tries to break the naan one-handed. She laughs a bit.* HARRY *laughs.*

BEN. He…

BEN *stares at* HARRY. *He looks upset. A while.*

He was called Adam. Our son. He was. So funny. Quiet. But funny, like you, he thought a lot. I used to think he hated us. His life, this place. I used to think he hated every single moment. And what torture. But I don't think he did, on the most part. I think he hated it that day. He hated everything that day. Just one day. One day. A year ago. She found him. In that tree, by the river, in his uniform. In that uniform.

HARRY *looks at* LOOPS.

LOOPS *stares at her outfit.*

I just wish it was me. I wish it was me.

HARRY. That (uniform)…

LOOPS *looks at her camo. Takes a while.*

LOOPS. They wouldn't let me join… Apparently I – I have… I have –

CAT. it's okay, darling –

LOOPS. I. Carry it. Him. I have – I can't – I had to do something else. I wanted to do something else.

HARRY. Something. Else –

LOOPS. …

HARRY. Me?

LOOPS. Harry –

HARRY. I… I'm sorry if this sounds… I, I need to – Am I here, because… Do I. Look like him?

LOOPS.…

HARRY. Louise –

CAT. No, Harry. You don't. He was… He was very different.

CAT *glances at the videos. A beat.*

HARRY. Okay… okay, I – I'm really sorry, but I'm gonna…

LOOPS. no –

HARRY. I'm sorry, I'm just – I don't think it's. Uh. Good. For me. Or – I'm gonna change (shirts). And then I'm… okay?

LOOPS *nods.*

HARRY *exits with his dirty shirt.*

The sound of insects is far quieter now. The numbers are dwindling.

LOOPS *goes to her mum and dad.*

She takes her camo jacket off, and hands it to CAT.

CAT *smells the jacket.*

CAT. Oh. Smells nice. Smells like you.

The sound of bugs fades away to silence.

BEN. I love you, you know. Both of you.

BEN *kisses* CAT*'s head. He kisses* LOOPS*'s head.*

HARRY *enters in the sick-covered shirt. He places the Villa shirt on the spare chair.*

CAT. Why don't you stay, Harry?

HARRY. Another time. Maybe.

CAT. Okay.

HARRY.…Uhm. I should… When-when you asked me, earlier, if if I saw. Your face, when I closed my eyes. Uhm… I… I just saw my mum. Very (clearly). And I have – *had* problems. With that. Too. So. So. Anyway. That's. Something.

HARRY *goes to leave.*

LOOPS. Harry... Just... uh...

HARRY. Lou, I'm really sorry, but –

LOOPS *reaches out her hand, shakily, towards* HARRY . *She points a finger. Carefully, she touches his left nipple.* HARRY *smiles, nods.*

Then LOOPS *touches his right nipple.* HARRY *nods. Then, carefully, her finger disappears into his belly button.* HARRY *smiles.*

The lights seem to hone in on them – circle them. CAT *and* BEN *almost fade.*

LOOPS. I'm in you.

HARRY. Yeah. You're my first.

LOOPS. cool.

HARRY. Nipple soulmates.

LOOPS. Told you.

I always liked you, Harry. I just. Never needed to do anything about it. Until today –

HARRY. Lou. You're crying.

LOOPS. What, no, I'm not.

HARRY. Yeah, you are.

LOOPS. Oh. Right. Is this crying then?

HARRY. It is, yeah.

LOOPS. Right, yeah. It's not all that, is it.

HARRY. Not really.

LOOPS. Can I kiss you?

HARRY. Yeah.

They kiss. It's much better than before. No shakes.

LOOPS. 'Kay, cool.

HARRY. What a day.

LOOPS. (Yeah.) Over now.

Outside, the first crack of sunlight – blood-orange, fading into black. Dawn. And the sound of new mayflies.

End.

www.nickhernbooks.co.uk

facebook.com/nickhernbooks

twitter.com/nickhernbooks